STILLNESS AFTER SHAHADA

Heart-Soothing Duas and Reflections for Muslim Reverts

Joyful Hijabi

Copyright© 2025 Joyful Hijabi

All rights reserved.

No part of this book may be reproduced or distributed in any form without the author's permission. This book is for inspirational and educational purposes and is not a substitute for religious advice from qualified scholars. First Edition - 2025 Printed in the United States of America

Table of Contents

Introduction 1
Chapter 1: You Are Not Alone 5
Chapter 2: Mindfulness in the Islamic Tradition.................................. 7
Chapter 3: Grounding Yourself in Faith... 10
Chapter 4: Mindful Habits for Daily Strength..................................... 17
Chapter 5: Your First Salah (Prayer) 21
Chapter 6: Your First Jumu'ah (Friday Prayer)................................... 26
Chapter 7: Your First Ramadan as a Muslim 31
Chapter 8: Your First Eid Without Family.. 36
Chapter 9: Your First Time Wearing Hijab 41
Chapter 10: Your First Test of Faith... 45
Chapter 11: Your First Doubts in Faith 50
Chapter 12: Your First Mistake as a Muslim 55
Chapter 13: Your New Family in Faith 59
Chapter 14: Your First Year in Islam 63
Chapter 15: Learning to Read the Qur'an 67
Chapter 16: Healing from Past Religious Hurt 73
Chapter 17" Building a Daily Du'a Habit 79
Chapter 18: Finding a Shaykhah or Mentor 85
Chapter 19: The Beauty of Serving Others for Allah's Sake 91
Chapter 20: Loving Allah When You Feel Unlovable 97
Chapter 21: The Journey Continues — And So Does His Mercy........102
A Gentle Whisper Forward 108

Introduction

To the one who chose Islam... and is learning how to breathe again.

You might be carrying a mix of peace and pressure—the peace of having found the truth and the pressure of figuring out how to live it. I've been there. Reverting to Islam is beautiful, but it's also lonely, confusing, and overwhelming sometimes.

This book is for *you*. Whether you've been Muslim for 2 weeks or 20 years, the mental and emotional side of the journey doesn't get enough attention.

What happens after the shahada? After the welcome hugs and takbeers fade?

That's where real life begins. And real-life needs tools.

I'm not a scholar. I'm someone who's walked the path. This book brings reflections, reminders, and practical exercises rooted in Islam to help you reconnect with yourself and Allah.

You don't need to be perfect. Just present.

Let's begin.

Welcome to the Journey

From questions to clarity. From confusion to peace.

I took my shahadah 25 years ago. On the outside, it looked like a quiet decision. But inside, it was a tidal wave of emotions, a turning point that changed everything.

I come from a hardcore Catholic family—the kind where faith wasn't just Sunday service but the backbone of life. My father was the Head of the Knights of Columbus, and my mother was the President of the Catholic Women's League. I was raised in that environment, attending mass every Sunday, singing in the church's choir, and even teaching Catechism to children. College days came, and then I studied at a private Christian university. Theology classes were part of the curriculum and lit a fire inside me that I couldn't put out.

I started asking questions.

Sincere ones.

Why did Jesus kneel and pray in the Garden of Gethsemane?

Who was he praying to?

If he was God, why did he ask, "Let this cup pass from me"?

Why did he say, "Father, forgive them"? Who was he speaking to?

The more I asked, the more the answers felt like riddles. I wasn't trying to rebel—I was trying to understand. I was soul-searching, not expecting to find anything outside of what I already knew.

I am always inquisitive about other faith communities. Around that time, I became curious about different religions—Hinduism in particular. My cousin introduced me to this ideology that God is Love and that all faiths evolve in love. I brought a picture of Ganesha into our home. I sang Bajans with our Indian friends, memorizing Indian songs of praise, doing the rituals, and believing in the reincarnation of God as a human being.

I was online one day, scrolling through early chat rooms on Yahoo Messenger, when I stumbled into a conversation with someone I assumed was Hindu. I had been reading about a figure called Sai Baba, and this person could tell me more. I bragged about my desire to visit India someday to meet this Sai Baba.

But as we kept chatting, I discovered the person wasn't Hindu. He was a Muslim.

I didn't know much about Islam back then. Still, this person started sending me verses from the Qur'an—verses about the creation of the universe—the Big Bang, the origins of life. Then he sent me Surah Maryam and stories of Jesus that stopped me.

They weren't strange or foreign.

They were familiar... but clear.

This was the clarity I'd been looking for.

That chat sparked something in me. I needed to read the Qur'an for myself, so I searched for a mosque—to find a physical copy. I wasn't ready to talk to anyone yet; I needed the book. And once I had it, I couldn't stop reading. The words felt like they were speaking directly to me, answering the questions I had carried in my heart for years.

That's how Allah guided me. Through a random chat on Yahoo Messenger when, I was searching for something entirely different. That's the beauty of this deen: when you seek truth sincerely, it finds you.

But even with that peace, the journey wasn't easy.

Reverting to Islam came with loneliness. Tension at home. Pressure to be perfect. A complete identity shift. Little by little, I realized that while people would hand you books on fiqh or how to pray—no one talked about the *emotional* and *mental* side of being a new Muslim.

That's why I wrote this.

This book is part story, part journal, and part companion. It's full of reminders, reflections, and practical tools to help you reconnect with Allah, yourself, and the path ahead. Whether you took your shahada last week or years ago if you've ever felt spiritually disconnected, isolated, or overwhelmed, this is for you.

You don't need to be perfect. You need to be present.

Let's take the next step together

Chapter 1
You Are Not Alone

Even when it feels like you are alone, Allah sees you.

After the shahada, there's a silence nobody warns you about.

It comes after the hugs, the congratulations, and the excitement of doing something brave and life-changing. It comes in the quiet moments when you're alone with your thoughts—wondering if you're doing things right if your family will ever understand if you'll ever stop feeling like a stranger in both worlds.

Reverting to Islam isn't just a spiritual shift—it's an emotional one. A mental one.

And for a lot of us, it comes with grief.

Grief for the old self, the old community, the old comfort zones. Even when you know you've made the right choice, it's still hard to let go of the life you knew.

And when you're surrounded by people who don't understand—or worse, actively oppose what you've chosen—it can feel like you're walking this path completely alone.

I felt it, too.

My family was silent about it. Being from a strong Catholic background meant Islam wasn't just different—it was seen as the opposite. The tension, questions, and misunderstandings built a wall between me and the people I loved most.

But here's the truth: **you're not alone. Not spiritually, not emotionally, and not practically.**

Allah is always with you.

He says in the Qur'an:

"Indeed, I am with you both; I hear and I see." *(Surah Taha, 20:46)*

This was told to Prophet Musa and his brother Harun when they were about to confront Pharaoh—someone far more terrifying than any awkward family dinner or cultural rejection. Yet Allah's promise was simple and powerful: *I hear you. I see you.*

That promise is for you, too.

You're part of a global family now.

Millions of people like you took shahadah quietly, online, through a conversation or a moment of clarity, navigating the same fears, struggles, and hopes.

You might not see them at your local masjid. You might not feel them in your city. But they're out there—and they get it.

The ummah is massive. And even if people fall short in welcoming you, **Allah already has.**

Chapter 2
Mindfulness in the Islamic Tradition

∽

"Presence is power. Especially when you're standing before Allah."

Mindfulness isn't new to Islam. Our deen is full of moments that call us to slow down, reflect, and return to the present. From making wudu to standing in salah, we are trained to pause, feel, and remember.

What is Mindfulness?

In simple terms, it's being aware of the moment you're in—without judging it or trying to run from it.

In Islam, that awareness becomes powerful when it's connected to Allah. It's not just "being present." It's being present *with purpose*.

Tafakkur (deep reflection)

Tadhakkur (remembrance)

Khushoo (humble focus in worship)

All of these are *acts of mindfulness*.

How the Prophet (peace be upon him) Modeled It:

He would pause before answering questions, staying calm even under pressure.

He told us to eat slowly, sit with our full attention, and speak only what's good.

He never rushed his prayers, even when busy with da'wah or battles.

He *lived* mindfulness because presence protects the heart.

Why It Matters for Reverts:

When you're new to Islam, everything is fast. Fast rules. Fast expectations. Fast changes.

Mindfulness lets you *breathe*. It enables you to grow at a healthy pace. It helps you:

Catch negative self-talk before it drains you

Feel grounded when life feels unstable

Connect to Allah in a deeper, calmer way

Quick Practice: Two (2)-Minute Presence Reset

Find a quiet spot. Sit. Breathe slow and deep.

Say:

Astaghfirullah (3x)

La ilaha illa Allah (3x)

Allahumma inni a'udhu bika min hammi wal huzn (1x)

Just sit. Imagine Allah's mercy surrounding you like a blanket.

3 Ways to Handle the Isolation Practically:

a. Create a "Safe Space" Circle

You don't need a big group—just 1 or 2 people who support your growth, even if they're online. Choose people who remind you of Allah, check in on you, and don't pressure you to be perfect.

b. Speak to Allah Like You're Writing a Letter

When no one else gets it, tell Him. Start a private du'a journal. Be raw. Be real. Make du'a feel like you're venting to your best friend because that's what He is.

c. Limit Energy Drains

Pulling back is okay if specific environments, people, or conversations constantly drain your spirit. Protect your peace. You don't have to explain your Islam to everyone—especially if they're not ready to listen.

A Du'a for When You Feel Alone

"O Allah, be my comfort when others can't. Be my peace when my heart feels heavy. Strengthen my steps, quiet my fears, and send people who remind me of You."

Say it often. Whisper it on lonely nights. Let it be your rope back to calm.

You are not alone. Not in this, not ever.

And as you grow—emotionally, spiritually, mentally—you'll begin to see that even the loneliness had a purpose.

It brought you here.

Chapter 3
Grounding Yourself in Faith

Because the soul needs more than knowledge—it needs connection.

Islam is more than just a list of do's and don'ts. And yet, when you're a new Muslim, it can feel like you're being handed an endless rulebook.

Learn how to pray.

Memorize these Arabic words.

Cover this. Avoid that. Don't say this. Don't eat that.

While these things *are* essential, if you're not spiritually grounded—if your heart doesn't feel connected—it can start to feel heavy, overwhelming, and even robotic.

You need roots.

Faith isn't just built through knowledge. It's built through connection.

Through presence. Through small, sincere moments with Allah.

Salah is Your Anchor

If you learn nothing else at first—*learn to pray*. Salah is more than a ritual. It's your direct line to Allah. And even if you're still learning Arabic or don't feel "spiritual" every time you pray, showing up is a form of worship.

Some days, all I could manage was standing, bowing, and whispering what little I had memorized. But even that brought me peace.

Start with what you know. Even just saying "SubhanAllah, "Alhamdulillah," and "Allahu Akbar" while standing in prayer counts. Let it grow with you.

Dhikr is the Medicine for a Heavy Heart

Remember Allah when your mind is racing, or your chest feels tight, not just intellectually but with your tongue and your breath.

Start simple:

SubhanAllah (Glory be to Allah) – when you're overwhelmed

Alhamdulillah (All praise is for Allah) – when you're grateful or need perspective

Allahu Akbar (Allah is Greater) – when something feels too big to handle

La ilaha illa Allah (There is no god but Allah) – when you need peace

Repeat these like a rhythm. Whisper them in your car, on a walk, or before bed. Let them replace the noise in your head.

Short Du'as to Keep You Grounded

"O Turner of hearts, keep my heart firm upon Your deen."

(*Ya Muqallib al-quloob, thabbit qalbi 'ala deenik*)

"O Allah, I ask You for peace in my heart and clarity in my path."

"O Allah, help me remember You, be grateful to You, and worship You beautifully."

(*Allahumma a'inni 'ala dhikrika wa shukrika wa husni 'ibadatik*)

You don't have to memorize them all at once. Pick one. Let it settle in your soul. Repeat it when you wake up. Or when you feel scattered. Over time, these short prayers become spiritual lifelines.

Breathe with Dhikr: A Grounding Practice

Here's a short breathing exercise that helped me during anxious moments:

Inhale deeply through your nose for 4 counts

Hold it for 4 counts

Exhale slowly through your mouth for 6 counts

While exhaling, softly say: *"La ilaha illa Allah."*

Do this for 1–2 minutes. It calms your nervous system—and more importantly, it ties your calmness to the remembrance of Allah.

A Du'a for Heavy Days

Spoken reflection. Soft, personal tone. It is designed to feel like a warm voice on a quiet, difficult day.

Take a breath, sis.

Deep and slow.

Let your shoulders fall.

Unclench your jaw.

Soften the space between your brows.

You've been carrying a lot.

I can feel it—even without words.

This… is for those days.

The ones where you feel off, disconnected, unseen.

The world keeps going, but something inside you is just… tired.

There is too much to say. Not enough energy to explain.

So don't.

Right now, sit with me.

Let's turn that heaviness into du'a.

You don't need fancy Arabic.

You don't need to be composed.

You need your heart.

Ya Allah…

You know what I'm holding onto.

The pain I've tucked away.

The loneliness I don't talk about.

The memories that still sting.

The fear of slipping, of not being enough, of being forgotten.

Ya Allah…

Wrap me in Your mercy today.

Make this weight feel lighter.

Give me a moment of peace that feels like a deep exhale.

Even if the world around me doesn't change—let something *inside me* shift.

Ya Allah…

I'm trying. You know I am.

And even when I fall short, I still want You.

Even when I feel numb, I'm still reaching for You.

Don't let go of me. Not even for a second.

Ya Allah…

Protect my softness.

Heal the places where I've been hardened by disappointment.

Bring back the joy that once felt natural.

Let me taste sweetness in Your remembrance again.

Ya Allah…

If this pain has a purpose, show me.

If this storm is shaping me, carry me through it.

If this is a test, help me pass it—with patience, grace, and my iman intact.

Breathe again, sis.

Soft, slow, steady.

Your Lord is listening.

Even when you whisper.

Even when you cry.

Even when all you can say is… *"Ya Allah, help me."*

That's enough.

You are seen. You are loved. And you are never alone.

The Qur'an is Your Mirror

When you open the Qur'an, you're not just reading a book—you're letting Allah speak to you. Even if you don't understand every word, the feeling it brings is real.

Some of the verses that grounded me in my early days:

"Indeed, in the remembrance of Allah do hearts find rest." *(Surah Ar-Ra'd, 13:28)*

"So, remember Me; I will remember you." *(Surah Al-Baqarah, 2:152)*

"Your Lord has not forsaken you, nor has He hated you." *(Surah Ad-Duhaa, 93:3)*

You don't have to feel spiritual to be spiritual.

Sometimes, you'll feel close to Allah. Other times, you'll feel numb. That's normal. What matters is that you keep returning, even if it's just one du'a. One sajdah. One verse.

Grounding your faith is about building that habit of *coming back*—over and over again.

Because Allah never gets tired of you.

Chapter 4
Mindful Habits for Daily Strength

Small steps. Big impact.

Reverting to Islam doesn't automatically make life easier. In fact, for many of us, it makes things more complicated—for a while.

But you know what makes it bearable?

What makes you slowly and steadily grow stronger from the inside out?

Habits.

Not big ones. Not "change-your-entire-life-tomorrow" kind of habits.

But tiny, consistent, mindful ones.

The kind that anchors you when the rest of the world feels chaotic. The kind that slowly chip away at anxiety, self-doubt, and spiritual numbness.

a. The 5-Salah Check-In

Every time you pray, take 30 seconds after tasleem to pause and *check in with yourself.*

How am I feeling right now?

Did I rush through that prayer—or was I present?

What's one thing I need from Allah right now?

You don't need a journal. Just close your eyes, breathe, and listen to your own heart. Salah becomes more than an obligation—it becomes a reset.

b. One Du'a Per Day

Pick **one du'a** and say it with intention at least once. That's it.

Write it on a sticky note and place it on your mirror or phone screen. Let it follow you throughout the day. Feel it. Talk to Allah like you believe He's listening—because He is.

Some examples:

"O Allah, expand my chest and make things easy for me." *(Surah Taha, 20:25–26)*

"O Allah, guide me and make me content with what You've written for me."

"O Allah, replace my restlessness with peace."

c. Tech Timeout + Dhikr Time

Take **5 minutes**—no phone, no noise—just you, your breath, and dhikr.

Try this rhythm:

SubhanAllah (33x)

Alhamdulillah (33x)

Allahu Akbar (34x)

Say it slowly. Let your body relax with each repetition. Let your soul absorb it.

Bonus: If you do this right before sleep. It changes the way you wake up.

d. The "Sunnah Sandwich" Habit

Attach a small sunnah to something you already do.

Example:

Before drinking water, say **"Bismillah"**

After drinking, say, **"Alhamdulillah."**

This small habit makes your whole day feel more *connected*. It's like walking through the world *with Allah*, not just trying to survive.

e. The "Shukr Snapshot"

Ask yourself:

What was one thing I'm grateful for today?

What was one thing I survived, even if it was hard?

Say **Alhamdulillah** out loud, even for the most minor things: a good cup of tea, a moment of laughter, a message that arrived at the right time.

Why Small Habits Matter

Because consistency *wins*.

The Prophet (peace be upon him) said:

"The most beloved deeds to Allah are those that are consistent, even if they are small." *(Bukhari & Muslim)*

Your habits shape your heart. Not just your schedule.

You don't need to do all five. Start with one.

Whichever one feels easiest or most meaningful to you.

Because when you build habits with Allah in the center, even the hardest days get lighter.

Chapter 5
Your First Salah (Prayer)

You stand on the prayer mat for the first time, your heart fluttering with nervous excitement. The room around you is quiet and still, bathed in soft light. You've just learned the words to recite – or maybe you have them written down in front of you – and now you raise your hands beside your ears. **Allahu Akbar.** God is the Greatest. Your voice trembles as you whisper the opening, and you wonder if you're doing it right. It's okay, dear sister... take a deep breath. This is your first Salah, and Allah knows it's new for you.

(gentle pause)

You might stumble on the Arabic words as you fold your hands and begin the prayer. Perhaps you only remember a small surah like *Al-Fatiha* or just a few phrases. Maybe you're speaking to Allah from your heart in English because that's all you can do now. Know that it's alright. Allah, the Most Merciful, understands every language, every word unsaid, every teardrop. What matters is the sincerity in your heart as you stand before Him for the first time in formal prayer.

You bow slowly, placing your hands on your knees. Your back is as straight as you can manage, and you say, "**Subhana Rabbiya** l-ʿ**Azim,"** – "Glory be to my Lord, the Most Great." The words feel foreign on your tongue, yet profound. Rising again, your mind races: *Am I doing this correctly? Did I recite enough?* Anxiety creeps in. But then you remember that Allah does not expect perfection from you, not now, not ever – He only wants your devotion. As you think of this, a slight smile forms on your lips, and you continue.

Now comes the moment that truly captures your heart: **sujood** – the prostration. You gently place your forehead and nose on the ground, hands by your sides. The carpet is soft against your skin. In that lowest position, you feel something unexpected… a wave of serenity washing over you. **"Subhana Rabbiya l-Aʿla,"** – "Glory be to my Lord, the Most High," you say, forehead pressed to the floor. And suddenly, tears well up. Here you are, a servant of Allah, in the most humble posture, yet your heart feels lifted high. It's a mix of awe and comfort – as if you've finally found where you belong: in conversation with your Creator.

You could pause a moment longer in sujood, letting the tears fall. In this private moment, you pour out your heart. You might whisper in English: *"Oh Allah, guide me, forgive me, I'm doing this for You."* Your voice cracks with emotion. You have never felt this close to God – so vulnerable yet safe. The floor collects your tears of relief, gratitude, and even the anxieties you carried into the prayer. You let them all go, pressing them into the ground and handing them to Allah.

(soft breathing sound, pause)

As you finish your first raka'ah (unit of prayer) and sit back on your heels, you feel your racing heart begin to calm. You continue to the next part, repeating what you can. Every movement is slow and deliberate; every word is a struggle and triumph. When you finally turn your head to the right and left to say the closing salaam – **"As-salamu ʿalaykum wa raḥmatullah"** – peace be upon you and the mercy of Allah – you are greeting the angels that surround you. At this moment, as you finish your first Salah, a gentle peace descends in the room. You have done it. You have completed your very first prayer as a Muslim by Allah's grace.

Sit there for a moment after the prayer is done. Feel the quiet around you. Your legs are a bit numb, or your tongue feels dry. Maybe you are overwhelmed and need to cry a little more. It's alright to feel emotional. This is a milestone in your journey, a conversation with Allah that you have longed to have. Stay in that moment of stillness. **Alhamdulillah** – all praise is to Allah – you whisper, thanking Him for guiding you here.

My dear sister, remember that Salah is a gift, not a burden. Initially, it might seem complicated – all the motions and recitations – but with each prayer, you will grow more comfortable. Soon, the very actions that felt awkward will become second nature, a source of comfort. In time, the prayer will become your refuge – the safe space you run to when you're scared, lonely, or grateful. It will structure your days and soothe your nights. It will be the anchor that keeps you steady through the storms of life.

Don't worry if you didn't get every word right or your mind wandered. Even lifelong Muslims sometimes struggle with concentration. What counts is that you're trying, and Allah sees that effort. He is **Ash-Shakur**, truly appreciative – every little step you take towards Him; He appreciates and rewards abundantly.

As you rise from your prayer mat, you might feel a new kind of happiness blooming inside. You just fulfilled one of the five pillars of Islam, establishing the prayer. You answered the call that your heart had been hearing. This was the first of many conversations you will have with your Lord.

Before you step away, take a moment to make a personal du'a. Du'a is informal, personal supplication – you can speak to Allah in any language or word. Raise your hands or close your eyes. Tell Him what's in your soul. Thank Him for this moment. Ask Him for strength to keep praying, to learn more, and to do it with love and sincerity. Something like: *"Ya Allah (O God), thank You for inviting me to pray to You. Please help me remember You always, help me perfect my prayers and let my heart find peace in them. Amīn."*

(brief reflective pause)

Congratulations on your first Salah, dear sister. Feel that calm? That is the stillness after shahada – the peace of a heart beginning to connect with its Maker. Cherish it. Whenever life feels chaotic, know that you can return to this state five times daily. You just have to turn to Allah, say "Allahu Akbar," and enter into the solace of prayer again. May Allah make your prayers the coolness of your eyes and the light of your soul. Ameen.

Chapter 6
Your First Jumu'ah (Friday Prayer)

The call to prayer – the adhan – echoes through the mosque's hallway as you step inside for your very first Jumu'ah. Your heart is pounding in your chest. The air is filled with a quiet reverence and a soft murmur of people finding their spots. You slip off your shoes at the entrance, just as you saw others do, and carry them nervously in your hand. Clutching them, you enter the prayer area. It's midday, the sun is glowing through the windows, and the carpet under your feet is plush. You whisper **"Bismillah"** – in the name of Allah – as you walk in, hoping you're doing everything correctly.

You look around, unsure where to go. Men file into rows at the front, and women gather in a section towards the back. A kind-faced sister catches your eye and smiles, beckoning you to sit beside her. Relief washes over you. You quietly say "Salam," and she warmly returns your greeting. Alhamdulillah, you are not alone. You settle in, sitting cross-legged on the carpet, trying to appear composed even as excitement and anxiety swirl inside you.

Soon, the Imam begins the **khutbah** – the Friday sermon. The hall grows still and silent. The Imam's voice is clear,

Joyful Hijabi

reverberating through the sound system as he praises Allah and sends peace upon the Prophet ﷺ. You recognize a few familiar Arabic words amid his speech – perhaps "Allah" and "Muhammad" – but much of it might be new to you. That's okay. You listen intently, head bowed in respect, letting the words wash over you. The sermon might be about faith, gratitude, or patience – you catch an English phrase that resonates here and there. "...have patience, for indeed Allah is with the patient." You feel those words are meant for you, calming your heart. You close your eyes briefly and slowly breathe, absorbing the advice.

(brief pause as the ambient sound of the Imam's voice fades)

As the khutbah ends, everyone stands up. It's time to pray the two rakat of Jumu'ah prayer. You also stand, following the lead of the experienced sisters around you. Shoulder to shoulder, you line up, feeling the sister next to you gently adjust your stance so there are no gaps between you. The Imam says **"Allahu Akbar"** aloud, and the congregation moves in unison. You bow when they bow, prostrate when they prostrate, trying your best to keep up. You're thankful that the Jumu'ah prayer is performed out loud by the Imam – it guides you through the steps without you needing to recite everything on your own.

You feel a profound sense of unity in sujood with your forehead on the ground alongside dozens of others. All around you, foreheads touch the floor before the One God. Different ages and backgrounds, but in this moment, all differences melt away. You truly feel the meaning of the Prophet's words, that the believers are like one body. Here you are, part of that body, part of this beautiful family of faith, all praising Allah together in synchrony. A tear slips down your cheek, dampening the prayer mat where your head rests. It's a tear of joy, of belonging. For the first time, you don't feel like "the new Muslim" or "the convert" – you simply feel like a Muslim, praying to Allah just like everyone else.

The prayer ends far too quickly. As you sit back and the Imam makes a closing duʿaʾ for the congregation, you raise your hands quietly and say *amin* with everyone. Your heart is soaring. You did it – your first Jumu'ah. When the congregation disperses, and people greet each other, a sister beside you turns and gives you a gentle hug. You shyly mention it's your first time attending Jumu'ah. Her eyes light up. "MashaAllah! I'm so happy for you," she says. "We're all sisters here – if you need anything, just let me know." In that moment, you feel an outpouring of gratitude. Perhaps this woman is a stranger, but she treated you like family in a heartbeat for no other reason than the bond of Islam.

Walking out of the mosque, you feel lighter, almost like you're walking on air. The world outside is bright and bustling, but you carry a serene joy inside you. **Alhamdulillah**, you think to yourself, praise be to God for this experience. The worries you had earlier – about where to go when to stand, or whether people would stare – all melted away when prayer began. Allah guided you through it.

On your way out, you notice a little bulletin board with flyers – maybe there's a weekly new Muslim class or a sisters' halaqa (study circle). You make a mental note to check it out next time. Knowing some resources and gatherings can help you learn and connect further comforts you. Jumu'ah was not just a prayer; it was a doorway. Now that you've stepped through, the path ahead in the community doesn't seem so intimidating.

My dear sister, your first Friday prayer is a significant milestone. The Prophet ﷺ said the best day the sun rises upon is Friday. By being here today, you've joined millions of Muslims around the world in a weekly tradition that goes back 1,400 years. Think about that – every Friday, everywhere in the world, Muslims line up just as you did, worshiping Allah in unison. You are now part of this grand story, this living tradition.

Before you leave the mosque, take a moment to whisper a duʿa of gratitude. Perhaps standing under the sky outside, you say, *"Oh Allah, thank You for guiding me to Your house today. Thank You for giving me sisters and brothers in faith. Please bless them and bless me with knowledge and companionship. Let me grow closer to You each time I come here. Ameen."*

(soft, reflective pause)

As you drive or walk home, bask in the afterglow of Jumu'ah. You might even notice that your heart feels more at peace and your mind clearer. That is the blessing of this day. Keep this feeling with you, and know that whenever Friday comes, you have a standing invitation from Allah to meet Him in the congregation. You answered that call today – and insha'Allah, you will many times more. May Allah always make you eager for Jumu'ah and make the masjid a place of comfort and belonging for you. Ameen

Chapter 7
Your First Ramadan as a Muslim

The new moon has been sighted – Ramadan has begun. As the news reaches you, your heart swells with excitement and a little nervous flutter. This will be your very first Ramadan as a Muslim. You've heard so much about it: the long days of fasting, the peaceful nights of prayer, the community spirit. Now, here you are, about to experience it for yourself. You whisper a quiet prayer: *"Ya Allah, please make this month a source of growth and blessing for me."*

Before dawn on the first morning of Ramadan, you wake while the world is still dark and quiet. You prepare a small **suhur** meal – perhaps a date and a glass of water or tea – and sleepily but gratefully partake in it, knowing this early nourishment is an act of worship, too. You whisper "Bismillah" and eat purposefully, savoring each bite as a blessing. When you finish, you take a last sip of water and glance at the clock, mindful that dawn is near. In that hush, you raise your hands in du'a': *"Ya Allah, give me strength for this day."* Moments later, the Fajr (dawn) call to prayer begins to echo – a gentle sign that it's time to stop eating and officially start the fast.

As the day unfolds, you carry on with your usual tasks – work, school, or caring for family – but everything feels different. There's a secret joy nestled in your heart: *I'm fasting for Allah.* The morning light feels brighter, and your purpose is clearer. Of course, there are hunger pangs that come and go. Near lunchtime, your stomach rumbles out of habit, and you smile to yourself, remembering why you're abstaining.

By afternoon, a wave of fatigue hits. This is when it gets tough. Perhaps you find a quiet moment to rest and whisper, *"Allah, keep me strong."* You remind yourself that fasting isn't just about food and drink but also about patience. When an annoyance pops up, you catch yourself. On a typical day, you might react, but today, you hold your tongue, remembering *I'm fasting.* You breathe deeply and let it go, seeking Allah's pleasure over momentary anger. To your surprise, the following calm shows that fasting is taming your hunger and character.

As the sun dips lower, the anticipation builds. You prepare a simple iftar for yourself – perhaps just water, a few dates, and maybe a warm bowl of soup. The moments before sunset are heavy with hope and prayer. You know the Prophet ﷺ said the duʿāʾ of a fasting person at iftar is answered. So, you pour your heart out: *"O Allah, I've fasted all day for You. Please accept it from me. Forgive my mistakes on this day and fulfill the prayers deep in my heart."* The sky outside glows orange and pink. Your mouth is dry, your body weary, but your spirit is aglow with eagerness.

Then – the sun finally sets. **Allahu Akbar,** you made it! With a grateful heart, you take a sip of water, uttering **"Bismillah"** beforehand. The water has never tasted so sweet, subhanAllah. You eat a date, soft and sugary, and feel the energy returning to your body. A wave of gratitude overwhelms you. You did it by Allah's grace – you fasted this entire day! Perhaps it's just you at your kitchen table breaking your fast alone, or maybe you went to the mosque and are surrounded by others. Either way, at that moment of iftar, you feel connected to millions of Muslims worldwide doing the same thing.

Night falls gently. After breaking your fast, you pray the Maghrib prayer, each word of al-Fatihah flowing with extra sweetness now. Later, you join the special night prayer of Ramadan – **taraweeh.** At the mosque, the Imam's melodious recitation of the Qur'an fills the air. You stand shoulder to shoulder with your brothers and sisters in faith, bowing and prostrating together. Even if you grow tired and only stay for a part of the prayer, your heart swells with devotion. Each word, each movement under the night sky, feels blessed.

Back home, you climb into bed with a heart full of contentment. Day one of Ramadan is complete. As you drift to sleep, you think about doing it all again tomorrow and look forward to it. It's incredible how the hardship of fasting transformed into a sweetness of faith by day's end. You feel closer to Allah, and a strange stillness settles in your soul, the peace you've sought.

With each passing day of Ramadan, you grow more comfortable with fasting. You even begin to cherish the pre-dawn suhoor and use the days to read a bit of the Qur'an. You notice your character improving – your words are gentler, and your heart is more compassionate. Truly, this holy month is training your soul in discipline and empathy, and you feel it with gratitude.

As the final days of Ramadan approach, you push yourself a little more, seeking the special blessings Allah has hidden in this month. One quiet night, you stand in prayer or sit making heartfelt duʿa' long after midnight. In the stillness, you feel an indescribable closeness to Allah, as if the gates of mercy are wide open. You ask Him to forgive you, bless you, and accept all your efforts. Tears flow freely, cleansing your heart in those precious moments.

And then, before you know it, the crescent moon of Shawwal is sighted – Ramadan is ending. There's a bittersweet feeling in your chest. You've fallen in love with this month – its serenity, its purposeful days, and sacred nights. Yet, there's joy, too, because the next day is Eid. You did it, dear sister. You completed your first Ramadan, subhanAllah. What a journey it has been – from wondering if you could fast a single day to finding the strength to complete an entire month of worship. On this final night, bow your head in gratitude. Offer a duʿa' from the depths of your heart: *"Ya Allah, thank You for carrying me through this month. Thank You for the strength to fast and the opportunity to draw near to You. Please accept my efforts –*

my prayers, my fasting, my charity – and forgive any shortcomings. Let the spirit of Ramadan live on in my heart throughout the year. Ameen."

(soft pause for reflection)

Your first Ramadan is a memory you will cherish forever. The lessons, discipline, and closeness to Allah have imprinted on your soul. As you prepare for the joyous day of Eid, smile, knowing that Allah is pleased with you and all the effort you have put into His sake. Insha'Allah, many more Ramadans await you in your journey ahead. But this first one – with all its wonder and struggle – will always be special. May Allah reward you immensely for every sacrifice you made, and may He allow the sweetness of this Ramadan to continue nourishing your faith. Ameen.

Chapter 8
Your First Eid Without Family

The dawn of Eid al-Fitr arrives with a mix of joy and an ache in your heart. You wake up early, remembering that this is the day of celebration after Ramadan – your very first Eid as a Muslim. You say **"Alhamdulillah"** for having completed the month of fasting. Yet, as you get dressed, you can't help but feel a hollow spot in your chest. You put on your nicest outfit (maybe a new hijab or a beautiful garment you bought for the occasion) and try to smile at the mirror, reminding yourself it's a day of joy – yet your eyes still glisten with tears.

Memories flood your mind unbidden. You suddenly recall Christmas mornings from your childhood: the excited footsteps running down the stairs, the twinkling tree lights, and the cozy scents in the air. The laughter of siblings or the voice of your parents saying, "Merry Christmas!" You remember the comfort of those traditions – the big family breakfast, opening gifts together, feeling so loved and safe. A lump forms in your throat as you compare it to this morning. Today, no family is knocking on your door, no parents are calling you to the living room, and no familiar holiday songs are in the air. Instead, there is quiet. A new kind of sacred quiet – the silence just after dawn, the whisper of **"Allahu Akbar, Allahu Akbar, la ilaha illallah"** from the Eid takbir you play on your phone. It is beautiful in its own way... but it feels so different.

You head to the Eid prayer, perhaps alone. Maybe a kind friend from the mosque offered you a ride, or you drove yourself. As you arrive, you see Muslim families everywhere – mothers fixing children's little embroidered outfits, groups of relatives taking photos in their Eid clothes. You smile at the scene; it's heartwarming but accentuates your loneliness. You quietly join the line for prayer. The Imam's voice calls out the joyous takbīrs, and everyone enthusiastically responds. You try to focus on the prayer – and for a few minutes, you feel joy. When you bow and prostrate on this morning of Eid, you thank Allah for letting you experience this day. *"Oh, Allah, thank You for guiding me to Islam and allowing me to see this Eid,"* you whisper in sujud. A small smile finds its way to your face as you utter the final salām of the Eid prayer.

After the prayer, people around turn to each other with cheerful greetings: "Eid Mubarak! Eid Mubarak!" Strangers hug and exchange smiles, and children run around with candy. You shake hands or hug a few fellow sisters next to you. For a moment, you feel a part of this big, joyful Muslim family. It warms you—these people barely know you but embrace you as one of their own on Eid.

Yet, as the crowd disperses, you find yourself standing alone again. Everyone pairs up with their families, heading home or to relatives' houses to continue the celebration. You stroll back to your car, the initial excitement of the morning waning into an acute sense of emptiness. What now? In past years, holiday mornings meant sipping cocoa and opening gifts with your family, immersed in togetherness. But today, your family isn't here. Maybe they live far away or don't understand this new holiday you're celebrating. Perhaps they even think your Eid is strange and has nothing to do with them.

Sitting in your car, you grip the steering wheel and allow yourself a moment to feel that sadness. It's okay, my dear sister. It's okay to feel a pang of loneliness today. Converting to Islam has filled your life with blessings, but it also meant some parts of your old life changed. Those Christmas mornings – you cherished them, and it's natural to miss them and the family unity they represented. Your love for your family hasn't vanished because you have a new faith. You allow yourself to cry and turn to Allah, asking Him to comfort your heart and reward your sacrifice for His sake.

(soft pause, sound of a deep breath)

After wiping your tears, you resolve not to spend this blessed day in loneliness. You may join other converts at a community Eid brunch or accept a kind invitation from a friend. If no gathering is available, you'll treat yourself kindly at home – cook a favorite meal, visit a nearby park, or call someone dear. Consider giving your family a quick call to share your love and tell them you're thinking of them. One way or another, you will find moments of joy today, insha'Allah.

As the day goes on, you do find moments of happiness. At the community gathering, perhaps an older Muslim couple greets you and insists you join their family for lunch – they sense you are alone and want to include you. Their genuine hospitality moves you. These little blessings patch the holes in your heart. You laugh a bit, eat something sweet, and realize that Eid can still be beautiful, even if it's different from what you knew.

By evening, you reflect on the day. It was a mix of joy, loneliness, nostalgia, and hope – and that's okay. You realize you can create new Eid traditions while cherishing your Christmas memories. Perhaps one day, your family will understand this holiday and even share it with you, or insha'Allah, you'll have your own circle of loved ones to celebrate with. For now, you did your best on this first Eid without them. You got through it and even found some genuine smiles along the way.

Make a du'a' from your heart on this night of Eid as you prepare for bed. *"Ya Allah, thank You for giving me the strength to get through this day. Please fill the void of my family's absence with Your love and with good companions in the future. Guide my family to understand me and let them see the beauty of Islam through my example. Forgive any misunderstandings between us. Bless me with many joyous Eids to come, surrounded by loved ones. Ameen."*

(gentle pause)

My dear sister, your first Eid without your family may have been bittersweet, but you showed great courage and faith. You found joy where it could be found and had patience where it was needed. Allah sees your sacrifice in giving up those familiar traditions for His sake, and He will not leave you empty-handed. In the Qur'an, Allah promises that for those who leave something for Him, He will replace it with something better. Trust that in time, He will fill your life with warmth and celebration that fulfill your heart. Until then, continue being kind to yourself. It's okay to feel what you feel. Know that you are never truly alone – Allah is with you, and your new Muslim family is here for you, always ready with open arms. Eid is about gratitude and togetherness, and you are part of the beautiful togetherness of the ummah. May Allah grant you many happy Eids and heal any loneliness in your heart. *Ameen.*

Chapter 9
Your First Time Wearing Hijab

This is the day you've been thinking about, maybe even dreading a little: the first time you step outside wearing a hijab. You stand by your bedroom mirror, fingers nervously adjusting the folds of your new headscarf. The fabric frames your face; it feels strange and comforting. In the mirror, you see a Muslim woman looking back at you – it's you, yet it's a new you. "Bismillah," you whisper under your breath, heart pounding. With that, you know it's time to face the world.

Walking toward your front door, the air is heavy with anticipation. Usually, leaving the house is mundane – grab your keys, step out. But today, it feels momentous. You pull the door open and step outside, hijab on. A cool breeze brushes against the parts of your hair now covered, and you clutch your bag tightly. Immediately, your senses heighten: *Are people looking at me? What will the neighbors think? Do I look okay?* A flood of self-conscious thoughts swirls in your mind. You can hear your heartbeat in your ears. But beneath the nerves, there's also a current of quiet pride – you are doing this for Allah, which brings a steadiness to your trembling heart.

You notice a few glances as you walk down the street or into the local store. Some are curious, some indifferent. In your mind, each gaze feels magnified. That older man across the street – is he frowning at you? The teenagers on the corner – are they whispering about your scarf? You swallow hard and stand straighter, remembering why you put it on. This simple cloth on your head is a statement of your belief, your faith, a symbol of modesty and obedience to your Lord. It tells the world, *"I am a Muslim, and I'm not ashamed of it."* Reminding yourself of that injects a bit of courage into your spine. You lift your chin slightly and continue.

Perhaps your first errand in hijab is just a quick grocery run. You grab what you need and head to the checkout. The cashier, who's seen you before without hijab, does a slight double-take, then smiles politely. "Have a good day," they say as they hand you the receipt – nothing extraordinary. You breathe out, realizing you'd been almost holding your breath the whole time. It turns out that most people are too busy with their own lives to pay much attention, a realization that loosens the tight knot of anxiety in your chest.

On your way back home, something beautiful happens. A woman passes by, also wearing a hijab. As she nears, she gives you a warm, knowing smile and says, "Assalamu alaykum, sister." It's just a simple greeting, but it feels profound. You return the "Wa alaykum salaam" with a shy smile. That one exchange fills you with a sense of belonging. It's as if, by wearing hijab, you've been recognized as part of a quiet sisterhood that was there all along, waiting to welcome you. You're not just a lone woman walking; you're visibly a Muslim woman, and other Muslims see you as one of theirs.

When you finally step back inside your home, you close the door and lean against it, exhaling deeply. You made it. The scarf is still snug around your head. Maybe it slipped slightly on one side or felt hot under the sun, but you managed. A wave of accomplishment washes over you. You think back to all the buildup of fear – the nights lying awake wondering how strangers or friends might react, the mirror practice tying your scarf repeatedly to get it right. And now here you are: you faced those fears head-on.

You walk back to your mirror, looking at yourself again. But this time, you feel a spark of joy instead of nervousness. You even laugh a little out of relief and pride. *I did it.* The girl in the reflection looks more confident now. She looks dignified. It dawns on you that the hijab isn't just an outer covering; it's changing something inside you, too. By choosing to wear it, you proved that pleasing Allah matters more than pleasing people. That realization makes your heart flutter with contentment.

Of course, you know not every day will be as emotionally charged as this first day. There may be days when someone says something unkind about your hijab, or days you feel lonely or frustrated and the hijab feels heavy. But there will also be days you feel incredibly grateful for it – when it gives you comfort, privacy, and a sense of identity. Today is a victory, and it's the first of many small victories to come.

Before you take off your hijab for the day, you sit down for a moment and make a duʿaʾ. *"Oh, Allah, thank You for giving me the courage to wear my hijab today. Please make it easy for me moving forward. Protect me from any harm or ridicule. Let my hijab be a light for me, a means of Your blessings, and a reminder of Your presence. Strengthen my iman (faith), so I wear it with pride and sincerity daily. Ameen."*

(soft pause)

My dear sister, wearing a hijab for the first time is a milestone in your faith journey. It's completely normal to feel anxious or afraid of judgment. But remember, every moment you wore that hijab today, the angels recorded your courage and devotion. You turned a page to a new chapter of outwardly living your faith. Take it one day at a time. Know that Allah is with you, and He is so pleased to see His servant choose His guidance over society's whims. There will be challenges, yes, but there will also be immense rewards. Every time someone smiles at you with "Assalamu alaykum," every time you pass a mirror and remember why you wear it, your soul will grow a bit stronger. You are a beacon of faith, and you're never alone – millions of Muslim women have taken this same step, and we are all cheering you on. May Allah keep you firm, make hijab a source of happiness for you, and reward you each day you wear it for His sake. *Ameen.*

Chapter 10
Your First Test of Faith

~~~

Not long after embracing Islam, you encounter something that shakes you. It might be an argument with a family member who can't accept your new faith, a close friend distancing, or a personal hardship. In that moment of difficulty, you feel the weight of being tested. Your heart, which was soaring with the joy of iman, now feels heavy, confused, and hurt.

One evening, for example, you might find yourself alone in your room after a painful argument with your parent. Their words echo in your ears: perhaps they said you've "changed too much" or that they "don't understand you anymore." Maybe they even insulted your new practices or accused you of abandoning your culture. Your cheeks remain damp from tears as you sit on your prayer mat, seeking solace. *Why is this happening, Allah? I thought after converting, everything would be peaceful...* you wonder. This is the first major trial you've faced as a Muslim, and it hurts deeply.

You remember hearing that tests are part of a believer's journey – that Allah tests those He loves to purify and strengthen them. But in the rawness of the moment, that knowledge sits in your mind like a distant theory. Emotionally, you feel shaken. It's okay to feel this way. Even the Prophet Muhammad (peace be upon him) and his companions faced immense trials and felt grief and pain. You are not alone, dear sister.

On this difficult night, you wipe your tears and turn to Allah with your anguish. You perform ablution, letting the cool water wash your face and calm you. Then you pray – perhaps two rak'ahs of voluntary prayer – pouring out your sorrow in sujud. In the stillness of the night, you whisper your duʿa': *"Ya Allah, I'm struggling. This test feels so heavy. Please give me patience (sabr) and strength. Do not let my heart waver. Comfort me and guide my family to soften their hearts. I trust You, Allah, but I need Your help to get through this."* Your tears fall onto the prayer mat, and you stay there a while, eyes closed, heart pleading.

After pouring your heart out to Allah, you feel a subtle sense of relief, as if you've been heard. The problem hasn't vanished – your family might still be upset, or the hardship is still real – but your heart feels just a bit lighter. You recall a verse from the Qur'an: *"And certainly, We shall test you with something of fear, hunger, loss of wealth, lives and fruits, but give glad tidings to the patient – those who, when afflicted with calamity, say: 'Verily, to Allah we belong and to Him we will return.'"* (Qur'an 2:155-156). You breathe those words in and try to internalize them. Life will have its hardships, but each difficulty is an opportunity to return to Allah and prove your faith to yourself and Him.

The test continues in the following days, but so does your resolve. You focus on what you can control: being kind to your family despite their hurtful words, gently explaining your faith when they're willing to listen, and seeking support from understanding friends or mentors in the community. Some moments are challenging – like when you overhear your mother crying because she worries she "lost" you to a foreign religion, or when you see friends posting photos out partying like you used to, and you feel a stab of loneliness. These are the moments that truly test your commitment. And through each of them, you keep reminding yourself: *Allah is with me. He guided me here, and He won't abandon me.*

You also remember that the Prophet ﷺ said, "The greatest reward comes with the greatest trial. When Allah loves a people, He tests them." This brings solace – your hardship is not a punishment but perhaps a sign of His care, a chance to rise in faith. Like the dawn breaking after a night, you notice your heart growing stronger. The pain hasn't completely gone, but you're more at peace now. You find yourself making more duʿāʾ, clinging tighter to your prayers, and finding comfort in the Qur'an. The test, while difficult, is actually bringing you closer to Allah.

One afternoon, you take a walk outside to clear your mind. The sun is warm on your face, and you breathe deeply. You realize that even though this situation is challenging, it has taught you how resilient your faith can be. A small smile forms as you think: *This test didn't break me. It made me turn to*

Allah more. Alhamdulillah, for even this trial. It's a bittersweet gratitude but a sincere one.

That night, you make sujud and thank Allah for guiding you through this first storm. You ask Him to keep strengthening you, to help you overcome every challenge with grace and faith. *"Oh, Allah, thank You for not letting me go. I entrust my affairs to You. Grant me patience in hardship and make me among the sabirin (patient ones). And please, soften the hearts of those I love and bring ease after this difficulty. Ameen."*

(gentle pause)

My dear sister, your first test of faith is never easy. But remember, just as gold is purified by fire, the believer is purified through trials. This hardship is not a sign of Allah's abandonment – rather, it can be a sign of His love, an invitation to draw nearer to Him. You endured this trial with patience and prayer, a tremendous achievement. Every tear you shed for Allah's sake, every time you bit your tongue instead of lashing out, every time you chose to trust Him despite the pain – it's all written with Him, never lost. The sweetness of faith often comes after it's been tested, and you will come out of this stronger, wiser, and even more compassionate. Take comfort in knowing that Allah sees every effort. He promises that **"indeed, with hardship will be ease."** (Qur'an 94:6). This ease will come, insha'Allah. When it does, you'll appreciate it even more because of what you went through. Be proud of yourself for holding onto your rope of faith. You are not alone – every believer faces tests, and our Lord is always near, hearing our cries and healing our hearts. May Allah lighten your burdens, increase your patience, and turn every hardship into a doorway to His mercy. *Ameen.*

Chapter 11
Your First Doubts in Faith

It's late at night, and you find yourself staring at the ceiling, your mind racing with questions you never anticipated. Since becoming Muslim, you've learned so much and felt such strong faith – but now, unexpectedly, you feel a flicker of doubt. Maybe you encountered something online – a criticism of Islam or a difficult question about religion – that unsettled you. Or perhaps the initial euphoria of conversion has worn off, and you're left with a quieter, more ordinary feeling, wondering where the excitement went. In this still darkness, a whisper creeps in: *"What if I'm not on the right path? What if I'm not good enough as a Muslim?"*

Your heart sinks at the presence of these thoughts. You almost feel guilty for having them. **"Waswasa,"** the whispered suggestions of Shaytan, often strikes when faith feels a bit low. But at this moment, it just feels like your own inner voice doubting everything you worked so hard for. You curl up on your side, hugging a pillow, as a wave of anxiety washes over you. *I've changed my whole life... what if I was wrong?* The doubt tugs at you, making you feel unsteady.

First, dear sister, realize that having questions or doubts does not make you a bad Muslim. Even some of the Prophet's companions asked questions to strengthen their understanding. Faith isn't a static emotion; it rises and falls. You're experiencing a dip – a test within your heart. Knowing this is actually a relief: you're not alone, and you're not the first believer to feel this way.

Instead of letting the doubts fester, you decide to address them. You get up, make wuḍū', and stand for prayer. Even though it's hard to concentrate, you push yourself to connect with Allah because you know He has the answers even if you don't. After praying, you open the Qur'an, seeking comfort. Your eyes land on a verse almost as if it was placed for you: *"It is He who sent down tranquility into the hearts of the believers that they would increase in faith along with their present faith."* (48:4). Tranquility in the heart – that's what you need right now. You close your eyes and ask Allah for precisely that: *"O Allah, send tranquility into my heart and increase me in faith."*

Over the following days or weeks, you take proactive steps to deal with your doubts. You seek knowledge if a specific question bothers you – like something about Islamic history or a difficult rule. You reach out to a trusted scholar or mentor or find reputable books or lectures for clarity. Each answer you uncover is like a brick, re-securing the foundation of your faith. If the doubt was more emotional – like feeling distant from Allah or unsure of your worth – you work on your spiritual connection. Even if small, you establish a routine of daily du'a' and dhikr (remembrance of Allah). You spend a few minutes each morning after Fajr reflecting on Allah's blessings, speaking to Him in your heart, and sharing your worries.

One morning, you wake up and feel a little spark of that love for Islam again. It might not be the dramatic rush of emotion you had on your Shahada day, but it's warm and steady. You realize that faith can be quiet and firm, not always loud and ecstatic. The doubts haven't completely vanished, but they've shrunk. They're like shadows now, present but not overpowering, because the light of knowledge and remembrance has grown brighter.

Crucially, you also learn to seek refuge in Allah from Shaytan whenever negative whispers come. You say, **"A'udhu billahi min ash-shaytan-ir-rajeem"** (I seek refuge in Allah from the accursed Satan) and follow it with positive action – read a verse of the Qur'an, recall a moment you felt Allah's help, or take a deep breath and remind yourself of how far you've come. These become your tools to push back the darkness when it tries to encroach.

As you go through this phase, you come to appreciate that iman (faith) isn't a simple on-off switch; it's more like a flickering candle you must protect from the winds. Sometimes, it burns bright and high; other times, it wanes and needs to be rekindled. Doubt was like a gust of wind—tightening, but ultimately, it taught you how to cup your hands around your flame of faith to shield it.

One night, after having weathered this storm of doubt, you make sujud and speak to your Lord: *"Ya Allah, You know what is in my heart. You know the questions and confusion I have. Please illuminate my heart with understanding and certainty. Increase my faith and remove any darkness of doubt. O Turner of Hearts, keep my heart firm upon Your religion."* When you sit up from that prostration, tears wet on your cheeks, you feel at peace. You've done what a true believer does: faced the questions, sought answers, and ultimately relied on Allah to strengthen you.

(soft pause)

My dear sister, experiencing doubt doesn't mean you're failing – it means you're human. True courage in faith is not to question but to seek the truth and hold on even when things feel uncertain. By confronting your doubts, you have strengthened your iman. Every answer you found, every duʿaʾ you made in desperation, has brought you closer to Allah. Remember, the Prophet ﷺ taught us a duʿaʾ for these times: "O Allah, place light in my heart." And indeed, He will. The fact that you care about your faith so deeply that these doubts distress you is a sign of iman in itself. The storm may come again, but now you have the tools and experience to navigate it. Always turn your heart to Allah – **"O Controller of hearts, make my heart firm in Your faith."** Keep seeking knowledge, keep company with those who remind you of Allah, and be gentle with yourself. Faith is a journey with ups and downs, but Allah will never abandon a sincere seeker. May He grant you unshakeable certainty and the sweetness of faith settled deeply in your soul? *Ameen.*

Chapter 12
Your First Mistake as a Muslim

It happened so fast. One moment, you tried your best to live halal; the next, you stumbled. Maybe you uttered a curse in anger, missed a prayer (or several), or fell back into an old haram habit you thought you'd left behind. A wave of regret and shame crashed over you as soon as it happened. *I'm a Muslim now; I shouldn't be doing this... How could I slip up like that?* Your heart sinks, and a gnawing worry creeps in: *Will Allah forgive me? Am I a terrible Muslim?*

On this day, you might be sitting alone with your head in your hands, replaying your mistake over and over. Tears prick at your eyes. You remember reading that when someone converts to Islam, all their past sins are wiped clean – a fresh start. But here you are, only a short while after, already making new sins. It feels crushing. In your mind, a whisper suggests: *"Maybe you're not cut out for this. Maybe you'll never be as good as those born Muslim. Why bother trying if you're going to fail?"* That dear sister is the voice of despair Shaytan loves to plant in our hearts.

Take a deep breath. This moment – as low and guilty as you feel – is a turning point, not the end of the road. Islam was never about being perfect; it's about continually turning back to

Allah, no matter what happens. The Prophet Muhammad (peace be upon him) said, "All the sons of Adam sin, and the best of those who sin are those who repent." This hadith is like a hand reaching out to you in the dark. It tells you that mistakes are part of the journey, and what matters most is what you do right after the mistake.

So what do you do now? You turn to Allah. With a broken heart and sincere regret, you seek His forgiveness – this is called tawbah. You drag yourself to the prayer mat and raise your hands, tears falling freely now. *"Ya Allah, I admit I did wrong. You know my weakness, and I'm ashamed. Please forgive me. You are Ar-Raḥman, the Most Merciful. You promised Your forgiveness to those who ask – so I'm asking, Allah. Forgive me and help me do better. Don't let me fall into this again. I need You."* You speak to Him as if unloading a heavy burden because that's precisely what you're doing. Each tear and each word of repentance is lifting that weight off your soul.

After pouring your heart out, you bow down and make sujud, staying there for a while. In that humble position, you feel the hardness of the floor against your forehead, and it grounds you. You're a servant of Allah who erred, but now you seek His mercy. And Allah loves to show mercy. The Prophet ﷺ taught that if we come to Allah with sins reaching the clouds but we repent sincerely, Allah will forgive us. He even said that Allah is happier with a person's repentance than a man who finds his lost camel in the desert after thinking it is gone – an analogy showing how joyful Allah is when you return to Him. Remembering this, hope begins to glimmer in your heart again.

Your eyes are puffy when you finally sit up from prayer, but your heart feels lighter. You say **Astaghfirullah** (I seek Allah's forgiveness) a few more times softly. A sense of peace washes over you – the kind that comes after crying hard and feeling comforted. You know Allah heard you. You have faith that He has forgiven you, as He promises in the Qur'an: *"O My servants who have transgressed against their souls! Despair not of the mercy of Allah. For Allah forgives all sins. Indeed, He is the Forgiving, the Merciful."* (39:53). You let those words soothe your soul.

Now, you pick yourself up and think about how to move forward. Yes, you made a mistake, but now you can learn from it. If you miss prayers, you make a plan to make them up slowly or to set a better routine so it doesn't happen again. If you fell into haram, you identify what triggered it – was it certain friends, stress, or being alone? – and plan to avoid or replace that trigger with a healthy habit. You remind yourself that one slip does not define you. What defines you is your effort to get back up and keep trying to improve.

Later that day, you look in the mirror. You see a servant of Allah who is flawed but striving. You whisper to yourself, *"Allah's mercy is greater than my mistake."* And you smile a little because you genuinely believe that now.

With a calmer heart, you make a du'a' before sleeping that night: *"O Allah, thank You for guiding me when I went astray.*

I know I will err again, so please always help me turn back to You. Forgive me for today's mistake and any I may commit in the future. Please grant me the strength to overcome my weaknesses and the wisdom to avoid the traps of Shaytan. Ya Allah, as You have promised, replace my bad deed with good as I repent to You. Ameen."

(gentle pause)

My dear sister, your first mistake as a Muslim is not the catastrophe you fear – it's a lesson and an opportunity. Feeling remorse is actually a blessing because it's a sign of a believing heart. If you didn't care, that would be a more significant problem. But you care deeply, which is evidence of your iman. Allah's door of forgiveness is wide open, day and night. Every single one of us needs that forgiveness again and again. So, never let despair take root. You've tasted the sweetness of turning back to Allah; keep that with you. There will be other slip-ups in the future – we're only human. But now you know the way: stop, repent, and try again. Each time you do that, you get closer to Allah, not farther. Remember, Allah loves the oft-repentant. So rise from this stumble with your head held high. You are Allah's servant, and He is the Most Merciful. No sin is greater than His mercy. May Allah keep you steadfast, protect you from hopelessness, and always inspire you to return to Him over and over. *Ameen.*

Chapter 13
Your New Family in Faith

In the months since your shahada, you've met a few fellow Muslims – at the mosque, in local study circles, or even online – who have become more than just acquaintances. They feel like family. At first, you were shy, unsure if you fit in. But slowly, you started forming connections. There's the friendly sister at the mosque who always asks how you're doing and invites you over for tea. There's the WhatsApp group of reverts where you all share your daily struggles and small victories. Bit by bit, you realize you are not alone – you have a new family in faith.

One day, you find yourself at a community gathering – perhaps an iftar in Ramadan or a weekly halaqa. You're sitting among a circle of sisters, listening to a discussion about the Prophet's life. As you glance around, you see women of different ages and backgrounds: some born Muslims, some converts like you, different ethnicities, but all united in their love for Allah. You share your reflections during the discussion and are a bit nervous about speaking up. Still, they smile and nod when you do, genuinely valuing your input. It warms you more than you expected. For the first time, you feel truly accepted as "one of the sisters."

After the event, a few of them hug you and say, "So happy you could join us, sis. We hope to see you again next time!" While driving home that evening, you reflect on how far you've come. Not long ago, you felt isolated, craving this sense of belonging. Now, Allah has opened a door for you to a whole new family – people who call you "sister" and mean it.

It's not only in formal gatherings, either. Think about when you were sick with the flu and one of the sisters from the mosque, whom you barely knew, dropped off soup at your doorstep after Jumu'ah. Or the time it was Eid, when a family in the community "adopted" you for the day, insisting you join their celebration so you wouldn't be alone. These gestures left you astonished – why would strangers care so much? But they aren't quite strangers, are they? The Prophet ﷺ said that the believers are like one body – when one part hurts, the rest feels it. You felt that prophetic wisdom in action through these caring people.

Building these relationships does take effort from your side, too. You remember pushing yourself to attend events even when you felt nervous, agreeing to join a weekend Islamic class where you made a good friend. You also made an effort to reach out – sending a message to check on that sister who looked upset last week or volunteering to help when the community organized a charity drive. With each small step, your bonds grew stronger.

You went from feeling like an outsider to a faithful member of the ummah.

Of course, like any family, not every moment is perfect. There may have been times you felt a bit out of place – maybe when everyone else knew Arabic phrases you hadn't learned yet or cultural customs at the mosque that were new to you. Maybe there were moments when someone unintentionally said something that made you feel different as a convert. But these instances became less significant as genuine friendships blossomed. Over time, you gain the confidence to ask, "Could you teach me that phrase? What does it mean?" And they happily do. You realize that most people are eager to help and include you, especially when they see your sincere interest.

One beautiful realization dawns on you: this bond of faith is special. Unlike your old friendships that were built on shared hobbies or school or work, these new friendships are rooted in a shared devotion to Allah. There's a depth and sweetness in that. When you get together, you chat about everyday life stuff – family, food, work –for sure. Still, you also remind each other to pray, or you end conversations with "Insha'Allah, see you soon" and "Fi amanillah (in God's protection)." These seemingly small things fill your heart with comfort. They are reminders that your connections now extend into the eternal – these are friendships that, by Allah's grace, can continue into Jannah (Heaven).

One night, you make du'a' for those who have become your new family. *"Oh, Allah, thank You for blessing me with* brothers and sisters in Islam. I was alone, and You sent me loving companions. Bless them, reward them for their kindness, and keep our hearts united in Your love. Help me be there for them as they have been there for me." As you say Āmīn, you feel tears of gratitude. You think of your biological family – you still love and pray for them dearly – but now know that family can be formed through soul connections.

(soft pause)

My dear sister, finding your place in the ummah (global Muslim community) is like discovering an extended family you never knew you had. You will continue to meet souls who resonate with and support you on this path. Cherish these people. Continue to nurture those relationships. Be that caring sister to others as well. The Prophet ﷺ said, "None of you truly believes until he loves for his brother what he loves for himself." You've seen what that love feels like now – the warmth, the inclusion, the empathy. Give it forward whenever you can, and it will return to you manifold. In moments when you do feel lonely or different, remember this family of faith is there – reach out and stay connected. You are a valued part of this beautiful mosaic of believers. Alhamdulillah, you found your brothers and sisters in Islam. May Allah always keep you surrounded by righteous companions, and may He make you a source of comfort and strength for others, too. Ameen.

Chapter 14
Your First Year in Islam

The seasons have come full circle. It's hard to believe, but it's been about a year since you said your shahada – since you took that brave, life-altering step into Islam. Tonight, you sit by your window with a warm cup of tea, gazing at the moon, and you let your mind drift over the past twelve months. Memories play like a gentle slideshow in your mind: the day you pronounced the testimony of faith with tears in your eyes, the first shaky steps of learning how to pray, the warm embraces of Eid, the quiet moments of doubt, the joyous discoveries and the complex tests. So much has happened in such a short time, yet your heart feels like it has lived a lifetime of transformation.

You recall the excitement of your early days as a Muslim—how every little thing felt new and meaningful—wearing the hijab for the first time and feeling like you were rediscovering yourself. Fasting through that first Ramadan, you experienced hunger and spiritual fulfillment intertwined. The first time you heard the Qur'an being recited, you felt it stir something profound in your soul. The sweetness of those initial iman highs was a gift from Allah to ease you into faith.

Then there were the challenges that followed. The moments you felt isolated from family or old friends, the times you made mistakes and sought Allah's forgiveness, the nights you cried out of loneliness or confusion. You faced each with courage, even when you felt afraid. You learned that Allah's promise is true – after hardship, there is ease. And indeed, ease came: in the form of a supportive friend, a heartwarming community experience, an answered duʿa' just when you needed it most, or simply a day when you woke up feeling peaceful and confident in your identity as a Muslim.

As you continue sipping your tea, you realize something profound: you are not the same person you were a year ago. Your faith has settled into your heart like a calm, steady presence. It's not always the fiery passion it was at the start, but it's deeper, more resilient. You've grown. You carry yourself differently now – with more patience and more purpose. You measure success differently – by worldly achievements, inner peace, and closeness to Allah. You have new priorities and dreams (perhaps you hope to memorize more Qur'an, help others find Islam, or raise a pious family in the future). And you have a reservoir of experiences from which to draw strength. When a trial comes, you can say, "Alhamdulillah, I got through something similar before, and Allah helped me then and will help me now."

It dawns on you that this year has been like a personal training program crafted by Allah. The highs and lows were all designed to teach you essential lessons: sincerity, patience, gratitude, and reliance on Him. You think of the verse: *"Did people think they would be left to say, 'We believe' and not be tested?"* (29:2). You've lived that verse and seen its wisdom. Through tests, your faith became real – not just words, but lived conviction.

A soft smile spreads on your face. You feel so deeply thankful to Allah for guiding you to Islam and guiding you through this first year. Many people experience a spark of faith but don't continue. Yet, here you are, still striving, still holding onto the rope of Allah. That is by His grace alone. *"Alhamdulillah, alhamdulillah,"* you whisper, your eyes moist with gratitude.

To commemorate this milestone, you decide to do something special. Maybe you pray two rak'ahs of extra prayer in the night, purely to thank Allah. Or you write a heartfelt journal entry addressed to your future self, describing this moment so you never forget how it feels. You may call that dear friend or mentor who helped you along the way and thank them for being part of your journey. You might even bake a little treat for yourself – why not celebrate? This isn't an official holiday, but it's your personal anniversary in faith and deserves recognition in a humble, meaningful way.

As you prepare for bed, you recite your nightly du'as and add one more: *"O Allah, I thank You for every blessing and every trial of this past year. Please keep my heart firm and my faith increasing in the years to come. Forgive my shortcomings and accept my efforts. Let me continue to grow closer to You with each day that passes. Make the next year of my journey even more fruitful in faith, knowledge, and goodness. Ameen."*

(gentle pause)

My dear sister, one year in Islam is just the beginning. Ahead of you, God willing, are many more years of learning, growing, and deepening your relationship with Allah. Take a moment to appreciate how far you've come. You went from a curious seeker to a devoted believer, from uncertain and anxious to more confident and serene. There will be more highs and lows, but now you know from experience that Allah's help is always near. Continue to build on what you've started. Keep seeking knowledge – there's always more to discover in our beautiful deen. Stay connected with your community and keep nurturing those precious bonds of sisterhood. And never stop making duʿaʾ, for a heart connected to Allah is the key to everything good.

You were reborn spiritually one year ago – today, you stand more mature in faith, ready to face what comes next. Trust yourself and trust Allah's plan. The road ahead is long but leads to the most magnificent destination: His pleasure and, ultimately, Jannah. Insha'Allah, every step you take will bring you closer to that goal. Congratulations on completing your first year as a Muslim. May Allah shower you with steadfastness, wisdom, and an ever-increasing tranquility of the heart.

Welcome to the rest of your beautiful journey.

Chapter 15
Learning to Read the Qur'an — Slow Steps with a Deep Impact

You sit in front of the Qur'an, fingertips brushing across unfamiliar script. The Arabic letters curve and dance across the page like secret codes. Part of you feels in awe... and another part feels deeply overwhelmed.

How am I supposed to learn this?

You're not alone in that feeling.

As a revert, learning to read the Qur'an in Arabic is one of the most humbling—and, at times, frustrating—parts of the journey. You might feel like a child again, struggling to pronounce letters, sounding out syllables like a first grader, unsure if your recitation is beautiful or completely off.

But here's something you need to hear right now:

Every syllable, every stutter, every drop of sweat on this journey is beloved by Allah.

The Prophet ﷺ said:

"The one who is proficient in the Qur'an will be with the noble, righteous scribes. And the one who reads it and stumbles

through it, finding it difficult, will have a double reward." (Bukhari & Muslim)

Double reward.

Not just for fluency. But for effort.

That means the days when you fumble through *Al-Fatiḥah*, stopping to breathe mid-word, guessing your way through *Al-Ikhlaṣ*, or blinking hard at a verse you've already recited ten times and still don't feel confident—that effort is not only valid, but also sacred.

You Are Not Behind

In the age of beautiful Qur'an recitations online and seasoned huffadh in the masjid, it's easy to feel like you're "behind."

But faith isn't a race.

You don't have to catch up with anyone. Your pace is the right pace for you. What matters is your **presence**, not your perfection. Learning the Qur'an is a spiritual act, not an academic one. You're not cramming for an exam. You're sitting with revelation. You're holding in your hands the exact words Allah spoke to humanity.

Even if your voice shakes.

Even if you forget how to pronounce "ḍād" every single time.

Even if you're still mixing up "thā" and "sīn."

Allah sees. And He loves that you're trying.

My First Attempt

I remember the first time I sat with a mushaf and tried to recite from the Arabic script. I had only just learned the letters, and I kept flipping back to the alphabet chart in frustration. My tongue refused to cooperate. I cried that day—not out of beauty, but because I felt defeated.

But later that night, as I wiped my tears and opened the Qur'an again, I whispered: *"Ya Allah, I'm doing this for You."*

That became my comfort: knowing that my efforts weren't wasted and that even my broken Arabic reached the heavens.

So, I came back again the next day.

And the day after that.

And little by little, something shifted.

I stopped trying to sound like perfect reciters.

I started reading for connection.

And the Qur'an slowly began to open itself to me—not just as a book, but as a friend.

Practical Tips for the Journey

Here are a few gentle tips that helped me, and I hope they'll help you, too:

- **One Ayah a Day:** Just one. Even if it takes you 10 minutes to pronounce it correctly, one ayah is still a step closer to Allah.

- **Trace the Script:** Run your finger under each word. Let the shapes become familiar, like tracing a loved one's handwriting.
- **Pair with Audio:** Use a slow reciter (like Mishary Alafasy, Mahmoud Khalil Al-Husary, and I love Saad Al-Ghamadi) and read along. Play, pause, repeat.
- **Repeat Out Loud:** Don't be afraid to hear your voice. Even if it quivers, even if it feels strange. Your voice, in remembrance of Allah, is beautiful.
- **Use Color-coded Qur'ans:** These highlight tajwid rules and help with visual learning. Some versions also transliterate Arabic for beginners.
- **Don't Compare:** Your path is sacred. Don't let the fluency of others make you feel behind. You are not behind—you are beloved.

On the Days You Feel Stuck

There will be days you feel frustrated. You'll sit with the Qur'an and stare blankly, unsure where to begin or feeling like you're not progressing.

Take a breath.

Close the book momentarily—not out of defeat, but out of reflection.

Whisper this du'a:

"Ya Allah, You sent this Book down for my guidance. Please make it a light in my chest. Open my heart to Your words. Let them enter, even if I struggle to pronounce them."

And then open the mushaf again—even if just to touch the page or to whisper *Bismillah*.

This struggle you're experiencing. It's a form of worship.

This slowness? It's intimacy.

This repetition? It's transformation.

What You're Learning

You're not just learning a new language.

You're learning **trust**.

You're learning **submission**.

You're learning to sit with something divine and say: *"I don't understand all of this yet, but I trust the One who revealed it."*

And that trust changes you.

It calms the mind.

It softens the heart.

It teaches humility, perseverance, and awe.

When Allah described the Qur'an, He called it a healing:

"O mankind, there has come to you an instruction from your Lord, a healing for what is in the hearts, and guidance and mercy for the believers." (Qur'an 10:57)

So let it heal you, even if you only read it one letter at a time.

You Are Part of a Sacred Chain

Every time you recite an ayah, you join a chain of believers who have recited these verses for centuries. Some with perfect tajwid. Others with trembling voices. Some in grand mosques. Others in hidden rooms.

And now... you.

A new link in this unbroken chain.

Your voice, your effort, your intention—it's part of the living miracle of the Qur'an.

So come back to it—every day, if you can, even for five minutes. Let it be your companion, your light in the darkness, your quiet reminder that you belong to something bigger than yourself.

Let it enter your soul—not just through your eyes, but through your ears, tongue, and heart.

And watch what it transforms in you.

A Du'a for This Journey

"Ya Allah, open my heart to Your words. Make the Qur'an a light in my chest, a comfort for my soul, and a guide for my path. Help me learn it with love and patience. Let every letter I recite draw me closer to You. I remember that even my struggle is seen and rewarded when I feel overwhelmed. Ameen."

Chapter 16
Healing from Past Religious Hurt

Some wounds are not visible on the skin.

They live quietly in the soul, tucked away behind polite smiles and polite salaams.

You carry them with you — to the masjid, into prayer, even into your new life as a Muslim.

Maybe you've never told anyone.

Maybe you've whispered, *"I love Islam... but I still flinch when I hear the word religion."*

That, too, is part of your story.

And that pain? It's real. It matters.

You Didn't Just Change Religions — You Inherited a History

When a person reverts to Islam, they don't just step into a new faith.

They step out of an old one.

And sometimes, that old one left bruises.

Maybe you were part of a church where love was conditional — where faith meant guilt, fear, or control.

Maybe you were taught that questioning is sinful and that your worth depends on your obedience to a person, not to God.

Maybe you were hurt by religious leaders, silenced when you asked hard questions or made to feel like a disappointment for simply wanting to understand.

You may have said *shahada* years ago, but pieces of that hurt still live in you.

It's okay.

Healing is not linear. And Islam is not a spiritual eraser.

It's a shelter—a space where you can finally exhale.

Allah Knows Your Whole Story

You don't need to pretend here.

You don't need to wear a brave face or say *alhamdulillah* when your heart is aching.

Allah sees the entire you — the parts that have healed and still tremble.

He is **al-Latif**, the Subtle and Gentle One.

He is **Ash-Shafi**, the Healer.

He is **al-'Alim**, the One who knows all things — including the scars you hide behind your hijab or behind your smile.

"Indeed, He is the Knower of the unseen and the visible, the Grand, the Exalted." (Qur'an 13:9)

Even the wounds that no one else understands... He knows.

Even the memories you haven't been able to speak out loud... He hears.

And He never turns away the broken-hearted.

Your Pain Is Not Proof of Weakness

It's proof that your heart is soft. That your past meant something. That your faith is more than skin-deep.

And even though that pain came from somewhere else, **you can bring it into your relationship with Allah.**

He doesn't say, *"Come to Me only when you're perfect."*

He says:

"Say, 'O My servants who have wronged themselves, do not despair of the mercy of Allah. Indeed, Allah forgives all sins. Indeed, it is He who is the Forgiving, the Merciful.'" (Qur'an 39:53)

That mercy includes your doubt.

Your distance.

Your disillusionment with religion itself.

When Islam Feels Triggering

Sometimes, even Islamic spaces can unintentionally stir up old wounds.

Maybe it's hearing strong religious language that reminds you of past manipulation.

Maybe it's a harsh voice at the masjid that reminds you of the pulpit where you once felt shame.

Maybe someone says, "Fear Allah," and you feel anxiety instead of comfort.

Please don't judge yourself.

Your nervous system is reacting the only way it knows how. And the most beautiful part? **Islam doesn't require you to deny that pain.** It simply invites you to turn to the One who knows where it came from.

Safe Spaces, Safe People

Healing requires space. And safety.

You are allowed to take your time.

You are allowed to ask questions.

You are allowed to say, *"That part of my past still hurts."*

Look for spaces where your story is honored, not silenced.

Seek out sisters who listen without judgment.

And if needed, consider trauma-informed therapy — especially with a Muslim counselor who understands both your spiritual and emotional layers.

Healing is not a betrayal of your past. It is the honoring of your soul.

Even the Prophets Were Hurt

You are not alone in this.

Every Prophet was tested by people who claimed to be righteous.

Even the most beloved of Allah were mocked, rejected, and ridiculed — sometimes by their own families or faith communities.

"And never came a messenger to them, but they ridiculed him." (Qur'an 36:30)

And yet… they kept walking.

They cried to Allah.

They asked for help.

They were human, like you.

You are not less spiritual because you carry wounds.

You are more tender. More real. More deeply connected to the mercy of Allah — because you have felt what it means to be broken and still return.

Healing Looks Like…

- Sitting quietly, whispering, *"Ya Allah, I still don't understand why it happened."*
- Crying during sujood and feeling like you're 7 years old again.
- Listening to the Qur'an and realizing it speaks to your pain better than any person ever did.
- Feeling anger toward religious institutions and still choosing to hold onto your faith in Allah.
- Lighting a candle, sipping tea, and journaling about the past — not to dwell, but to let it go.

You Are Not a Failure Because You Still Feel Hurt

Sometimes, we believe that being "strong in iman" means not feeling sadness, anxiety, or resentment. But that's not strength. Strength is kneeling in the dark and whispering,

"Ya Allah, I still believe in You even when I'm confused. Even when I hurt. I still believe."

And that whisper is more powerful than a thousand speeches.

A Du'a for Healing

"Ya Allah, I carry pain from the past. Some of it still hurts. Please heal me with Your light. Replace bitterness with peace, fear with trust, and scars with wisdom. Surround me with people who remind me of Your mercy. Could you show me the beauty of faith gently? And never let me confuse You with the ones who hurt me. Ameen."

Chapter 17
Building a Daily Du'a Habit

There is something sacred about the whispered words no one else hears.

The ones you say under your breath while doing the dishes.

The ones you write in your notebook but never show anyone.

The ones you cry into your pillow at night when the world feels too heavy.

These are your du'as.

And they are not small.

They are not lost.

They are not forgotten.

They rise.

They travel.

They reach the One who always listens.

"And your Lord says, 'Call upon Me; I will respond to you.'" (Qur'an 40:60)

This isn't a poetic invitation. It's a promise.

Du'a Is More Than Asking — It's Belonging

Sometimes, people think du'a is only for big things: illness, marriage, job interviews, disasters.

But du'a is much more than asking for outcomes.

It's how we remember that we are held.

It's how we connect to Allah in the middle of the ordinary.

It's how we belong — even when we feel like outsiders in this world.

You don't have to wait until you've performed perfect wudu or are sitting on a prayer mat to talk to Allah.

He is near. Always.

In traffic. In the shower. While folding laundry. While rocking a baby to sleep.

In fact, the best time to make du'a is often when you feel the least "ready."

Because it's in that rawness — that realness — that your heart is most open.

Du'a Is the Language of the Soul

As a revert, you might feel uncertain about how to make du'a.

Maybe you think, *"I don't know the Arabic words. Will Allah still understand me?"*

The answer is yes. A thousand times, yes.

Allah understands every language. Every tear. Every thought you haven't even spoken yet.

You can talk to Him in English, Tagalog, Spanish, Swahili — whatever language your heart thinks in. Du'a is not about eloquence. It's about sincerity.

"Verily, your Lord is shy and generous. He is shy when His servant raises his hands to Him to return them empty." (Ahmad)

Raise your hands.

Whisper what you're feeling.

Write what you can't say out loud.

He is listening.

Start Small, Stay Close

Here are a few gentle ways to make du'a part of your daily rhythm:

- **Wake-up whisper:**
- "Ya Allah, thank You for waking me up. Guide me today. Protect me from what I can't see."
- **While driving or walking:**
- "Ya Allah, keep me safe. Bring ease to someone who is struggling today."
- **Before sleep:**
- "Forgive me, Ya Rabb. I tried. Hold me while I rest. Help me try again tomorrow."

- **When anxious:**
- "Ya Allah, calm my heart. Replace this fear with Your peace."

You don't need to recite long formal supplications — though those are beautiful too. Just speak. Speak from your soul. Speak like you're sitting across from someone who loves you more than anyone ever could.

Because you are.

Du'a Is Not Always for Change — Sometimes It's for Closeness

Yes, we ask Allah for what we need — health, guidance, help, forgiveness.

But du'a also softens us.

When you speak to Allah throughout your day, something shifts inside you. You feel less alone. Less frantic. More rooted.

Du'a reminds you that you don't have to carry everything by yourself.

You are not in control of the world — and that is a relief, not a burden.

Du'a doesn't always change the situation. But it always changes **you**.

It transforms fear into hope.

Sadness into surrender.

Confusion into connection.

A Du'a Notebook for the Soul

One of the most healing things I ever started was a "du'a journal." Nothing fancy. Just a little notebook I kept beside my bed.

Every night, I'd write a sentence or two:
- "Ya Allah, help me learn to forgive."
- "Please protect my parents, even though they're not Muslim yet."
- "Show me where I'm needed."
- "Don't let my loneliness make me forget You."

Months later, I looked back and realized that some of those du'as had already been answered.

And others? They were answered in ways I didn't expect.

The beauty of writing du'as is that it slows you down. It helps you notice your needs, your fears, your dreams — and hand them all over to the One who already knows.

Try it. One line a day.

You might be surprised how your relationship with Allah deepens — quietly, gently, steadily.

Du'a When You Don't Know What to Say

There will be days when your heart feels too tired to form words. That's okay.

You can just sit.

You can cry.

You can say, "Ya Allah," and let the silence carry the rest.

He understands what's behind your silence.

Sometimes, the most powerful du'a is just **showing up**.

Just lifting your hands. Just whispering His name.

"And He is with you wherever you are." (Qur'an 57:4)

What Happens After Du'a?

You wait. You trust. You let go.

Du'a is not a vending machine. It's a surrender.

And the answer isn't always "yes."

Sometimes it's "not yet."

Sometimes it's "I have something better."

Sometimes it's "I'm saving it for your akhirah."

But there is **always** a response — even if it's in the form of peace, clarity, or a door you didn't expect to open.

A Du'a to Begin (or Begin Again)

"Ya Allah, make Your remembrance sweet on my tongue and constant in my heart. Let du'a become my anchor. Make me someone who turns to You in the morning, in the quiet, chaos, and joy. Remind me that You are near, always near. Ameen."

Chapter 18
Finding a Shaykhah or Mentor

There are days on this path when your heart feels like it's floating — full of love for Allah, full of light, full of certainty.

And there are other days…

When you feel unsure.

You hesitate before praying.

You wonder if you're "doing it right."

You're not even sure which questions you're allowed to ask.

It can feel like you're walking this road alone in those moments.

But Islam was never meant to be a solo journey.

Even the Prophet ﷺ was surrounded by companions. People he taught, laughed with, wept with. People who asked him questions — sometimes awkward ones, sometimes obvious ones, sometimes profound ones.

And he answered them with mercy.

That's what a mentor can be for you — someone to walk with you, not ahead of you. Someone who reminds you that your questions are not a burden. That your growth matters. That you are not alone.

What Is a Shaykhah or Mentor Really?

You might hear the word "shaykhah" and imagine a highly educated female scholar, fluent in Arabic and trained in Islamic jurisprudence. And yes — those women exist, and their knowledge is precious.

But your mentor doesn't need to be a scholar to be meaningful.

She can be a sister who's walked this path a few years longer.

A revert who remembers what it felt like to struggle through wudu.

A teacher who explains things without making you feel small.

Even a kind-hearted auntie who checks in on you and prays for you.

Mentorship isn't about status — it's about sincerity.

The Prophet ﷺ said:

"The best of you are those who learn the Qur'an and teach it." (Bukhari)

That includes the sister who helps you pronounce your surahs, the friend who shows you how to do sujood, or the teacher who patiently answers your late-night texts about fasting.

Why It Matters

When you have a safe, spiritually grounded mentor, a few beautiful things happen:

- You feel **less alone**.
- You gain **clarity** without feeling judged.
- You receive **support** that's based on the Qur'an and Sunnah — not just opinions.
- You build a **spiritual friendship** rooted in sincerity.

And maybe most importantly:

You realize that seeking help is not weakness — it's **wisdom**.

The Prophet ﷺ never dismissed a questioner. He never made someone feel silly for not knowing. That tradition of gentleness continues through good mentors.

How to Find a Mentor (When It Feels Impossible)

Let's be honest — it's not always easy.

Some communities are small.

Some masjids don't have female teachers.

Some spaces feel intimidating — especially if you're a new Muslim who doesn't "look the part."

Here are a few gentle places to begin:

- **Ask at your local masjid** if there's a convert support group or women's study circle.
- **Attend Islamic classes or halaqas** and notice who seems approachable and kind.
- **Explore online spaces** like Seekers Guidance, AlMaghrib Institute, Rabata, or local Muslim women's groups.

- **Ask Allah directly.** Before any of this, whisper:
- *"Ya Allah, send me someone to help me grow closer to You."*

I did this once — right after feeling especially lost. Two weeks later, I was invited to a small Qur'an circle with a gentle older sister who became like a mother to me. She wasn't flashy. She wasn't famous. But her character was radiant. And her guidance was sincere.

What to Look For in a Shaykhah or Mentor

- **Mercy** — does she lead with compassion, or with criticism?
- **Knowledge** — not just book knowledge, but wisdom in how she applies it.
- **Humility** — she admits what she doesn't know and encourages you to seek the truth.
- **Boundaries** — she respects your time, space, and journey.
- **Sincerity** — you feel closer to Allah after talking to her, not just closer to her.

And remember no one is perfect. Mentors are humans too. They are not your replacement for Allah — they support your path *to* Allah.

When You've Been Let Down

Sometimes, we place our hope in someone we admire — and then feel hurt when they disappoint us. Maybe they were harsh.

Maybe they ghosted you. Perhaps they weren't who you thought they were.

Please know that experience doesn't invalidate the value of mentorship. It just means that person wasn't the right guide for your soul.

And it's okay to step away. It's OK to protect your peace.

Even the most beautiful gardens sometimes have thorns.

Keep seeking. The right teacher will come.

And until then — Allah is still nearby.

"And We have already sent messengers among the former peoples before you."

"And there never came to them a messenger, but they ridiculed him." (Qur'an 36:30)

Even prophets were misunderstood.

Even the sincerest messengers faced rejection.

So, if you've felt unseen — you're in good company.

You Might Be a Mentor One Day, Too

Yes, you.

The one still learning surah Fatimah.

The one still Googling how to make up missed fasts.

The one who cries during wudu because it still feels unfamiliar.

One day, inshaAllah, you'll be the sister someone else looks up to.

You'll be the one they come to with trembling questions.

And because you remember how it felt, you'll answer with gentleness.

You won't need to be perfect.

You'll just need to be sincere.

And that sincerity? That's the real legacy of the Prophet ﷺ.

A Du'a for Guidance Through Others

"Ya Allah, bless me with righteous mentors who teach with mercy. Let them be a light in my life and help me become a light for others. Surround me with people who remind me of You. And never let me forget: You are my first and forever Teacher." Ameen.

Chapter 19
The Beauty of Serving Others for Allah's Sake

A special kind of healing happens when you help someone — not for a thank you, not for recognition, but purely for the sake of Allah.

It can be something small. Almost invisible to others.

Like handing a tired sister a plate of food at the masjid.

Like texting someone just to check on their heart.

Like cleaning up quietly after an event when everyone else has left.

These acts might seem simple — but to Allah, they are acts of love.

And for the one who gives, they can be moments of healing.

Why Service Matters in Islam

As a revert, you may have already done the hard work of letting go of your old habits, your old life, and your old identity. Sometimes, what comes next is the ache of *now what?*

What does a life of ibadah (worship) really look like?

Of course, it includes prayer and fasting and Qur'an — but it also includes acts of service. Quiet, beautiful acts that make someone else's life easier.

The Prophet ﷺ said:

"The most beloved of people to Allah are those who are most beneficial to others."

(al-Mu'jam al-Awsat)

And that doesn't mean grand charity projects or public speeches. It means you, in your own small corner of the world, looking around and asking:

"Who can I help today?"

You Are Already Enough

Before you start to think, *But I don't know enough yet,* or *I'm still learning myself,* please remember this:

Service is not reserved for scholars.

It is not limited to those who've memorized the Qur'an.

You don't need a title or a platform.

You just need a willing heart.

Your hugs, your smile, your presence, your lived experience as a revert — that is *already* a form of da'wah. A form of service.

The Prophet ﷺ said:

"Even a smile is charity." (Muslim)

So don't underestimate what you bring to the ummah.

Your kindness is needed.

Your story is needed.

Your gentle reminders are needed.

When You Serve, You Heal

Sometimes, we focus so much on our own emotional wounds that we forget the power of helping someone else carry theirs.

There's something divine about that.

You might be grieving — and then you deliver food to a new mother, and it softens something inside of you.

You might be feeling lonely, but then you offer a ride to a sister who needs one, and suddenly, you feel connected again.

Helping others for Allah's sake is not just a gift to them.

It's a gift to you, too.

Because every time you give something in secret — your time, energy, and compassion — Allah gives something back to you.

Maybe not in the same form. But always in a better one.

Simple Ways to Start Serving

You don't need to wait for a formal opportunity. Just start with what's in front of you:

- Smile and greet your sisters with warmth at the masjid.
- Offer to help clean up after a gathering.
- Bring tea to an elderly neighbor.
- Babysit a revert sister's kids so she can go to a class or take a break.

- Donate a few dollars toward a cause — even if it's small.
- Share a kind word with someone who looks left out.

The most beloved actions to Allah are not necessarily the biggest.

They are the most **consistent** — and the sincerest.

"Do not belittle any good deed, even meeting your brother with a cheerful face." (Muslim)

Service Without Expectation

One of the most challenging but most liberating parts of service is this:

Do it only for Allah.

Not for likes.

Not for validation.

Not even for thank you's.

Because when you serve for His sake alone, disappointment disappears.

You're not waiting to be seen — you're already seen by the One who matters most.

Allah records it all—the effort, the sacrifice, the pure intention, the tiny moment no one noticed but Him.

"Whatever good you put forward for yourselves — you will find it with Allah." (Qur'an 2:110)

Every dish you washed for someone else.

Every ride you gave.

Every secret du'a you made for someone in pain.

It's all written. It's all reward.

Even the Prophet ﷺ Served

The Prophet ﷺ didn't sit above his community. He served them.

He mended his own clothes, cleaned the house, visited the sick, carried things for the elderly, comforted the brokenhearted, stood with the oppressed, and made people feel seen.

And he taught us that leadership, piety, and closeness to Allah are found not in control — but in **compassion**.

You follow in his footsteps every time you serve someone with gentleness.

Your Story Is a Gift

As a revert, you may not realize how impactful your presence is.

You remind others of the gift of guidance.

You bring a fresh perspective.

You offer lived wisdom.

You connect with others who are still searching.

Every time you welcome someone new with a hug, or share your story with honesty, or encourage a struggling sister with your warmth — you're doing da'wah.

Not the loud kind.

The kind that touches hearts quietly and permanently.

You don't need to quote hadith to be a blessing in someone's life.

Sometimes, your sincerity is the message.

A Du'a for Service

"Ya Allah, use me for Your sake. Let my hands help, my words heal, and my presence bring comfort. Accept every act I do in secret for You. Let me be a source of peace, not pride. A means of mercy, not harm. And when I give, let it bring me closer to You. Ameen."

Chapter 20
Loving Allah When You Feel Unlovable

Some days, your faith feels like light.

On other days, it feels like weight.

You wake up late and miss Fajr.

You snap at someone you love.

You forget to say bismillah before eating.

You scroll past reminders of Jannah and feel nothing.

And somewhere in your heart, a whisper rises:

"Maybe I'm not good enough for Allah."

It's a painful thought—a heavy one.

But you're not the only one who's felt it.

We all go through it — especially those of us who came to Islam from a background of guilt-based religion or spiritual shame. We were taught to fear God but not to love Him. To perform, but never to feel held.

But Islam is different.

Yes, Allah is Just. Yes, He is Majestic.

But He is also **Ar-Rahman**, the Most Compassionate.

Ar-Raheem, the Most Merciful.

Al-Wadud, the Most Loving.

"Indeed, those who believe and do righteous deeds — the Most Merciful will appoint for them love." (Qur'an 19:96)

Yes, **love.**

Allah's love is not reserved for the perfect.

It's for the returning.

You're Allowed to Come as You Are

You don't need to be spiritually "put together" to come to Allah.

You don't need a flawless salah record.

You don't need a polished hijab.

You don't need to know all the du'as or pronounce every letter with tajwid.

You just need a heart that wants Him.

That's enough.

The Prophet ﷺ said:

"Allah says: 'Whoever comes to Me walking, I will come to him running.'" (Bukhari)

That's not the promise of a harsh judge.

That's the promise of a loving Lord.

He didn't say: "Whoever comes to Me *perfectly*, I will accept."

He said: *"Just come."*

When You Feel Spiritually Ugly

We all have days when we feel messy, distant, impure.

The sin feels too big.

The habit feels too hard to break.

The guilt feels too sharp.

And Shaytan whispers: *"Why even try? Allah wouldn't want you now."*

But Shaytan is a liar.

He wants you to run *away* from Allah — when you should be running *to* Him.

Remember this:

"O My servants who have transgressed against themselves, do not despair of the mercy of Allah. Indeed, Allah forgives all sins." (Qur'an 39:53)

All sins. Not some. Not only the small ones.

All.

Even yours. Even mine.

Faith Isn't Always a Feeling

There will be days when you don't feel "in love" with Allah — just like there are days you don't feel "in love" with yourself.

But feelings are not facts.

Your love for Allah can be quiet. Tired. Even numb.

But the fact that you miss Him? The fact that you *want* to feel closer.

That's love.

Iman fluctuates. That's not a flaw. That's human.

The Prophet ﷺ said:

"Every heart has its ups and downs. So, if it's inclined to goodness, be hopeful. And if it's inclined to evil, turn back to Allah and seek His mercy." (Tirmidhi)

You are not unlovable. You are simply in need of mercy.

And mercy is what Allah gives most.

The Day I Felt Unworthy

There was a time early in my Islam when I felt like a failure. I had just broken a promise I made to myself about improving my prayers. I cried on the prayer mat, feeling so far from Allah.

And I remember whispering, *"I'm sorry, Ya Rabb. I don't know why I keep messing up."*

There was no lightning bolt. No miracle. Just a gentle warmth in my heart — the kind that says, *"I still hear you."*

And that's when I realized Allah doesn't stop loving you when you stumble. He stays. Waiting. Hoping. Calling you back with gentleness.

Not because of your deeds — but because of **His** love.

What If I Can't Love Myself?

You might think, *"How can Allah love me if I don't even love myself?"*

But here's the truth: Allah's love isn't based on your self-esteem.

He doesn't love you because you're confident or pious or polished.

He loves you because He **created you.**

He knows you.

He chose you for Islam.

And He sees the soft parts of you that no one else does.

Even on the days you can't stand yourself — He still sees beauty in you.

And He never grows tired of you, even when you're tired of yourself.

A Practice for the Days You Feel Unlovable

- Sit in silence. Place your hand over your heart.
- Whisper: *"Ya Allah, I'm trying." Even if you feel like you're not.
- Write down three things you've done — no matter how small — that show you're turning toward Him.
- Read one verse from the Qur'an that reminds you of mercy.
- End with this du'a:

"Ya Allah, love me when I struggle to love myself. Be patient with my soul when I am not. Remind me that I am worthy of You — not because I'm perfect, but because You are Ar-Rahman. The Most Merciful."

Chapter 21

The Journey Continues — And So Does His Mercy

You've made it to the final chapter.

But this?

This is not the end.

This is just a pause, a breath, a quiet reminder that your journey with Allah is just beginning.

You may have taken your shahada weeks ago, or years ago.

You may have prayed your first salah recently, or you're still building the habit.

You may be in love with the deen — or still learning how to feel connected to it.

Wherever you are, you are still walking.

Still breathing faith.

Still trying.

And that trying? It matters.

To Allah, it always matters.

"Indeed, those who have said, 'Our Lord is Allah' and then remained steadfast — the angels descend upon them..." (Qur'an 41:30)

Not those who were flawless.

Not those who were always strong.

But those who remained *steadfast*.

Who kept going? Who stood back up. Who whispered *"Ya Allah"* even when their voice trembled.

That's you.

This Book May Be Ending — But Your Path Is Not

You've cried through some of these pages.

You've nodded silently while reading a reflection that felt like it was written just for you.

You've whispered a du'a you didn't know you needed.

You've realized that your struggles are valid, your faith is evolving, and your place in the ummah is real.

You are not an outsider anymore.

You're not "still new."

You're a Muslim — a beloved servant of Allah.

And He has been walking beside you every step of the way.

When you were nervous at your first masjid visit… He was with you.

When you couldn't pronounce Al-Fatihah but tried anyway… He was listening.

When you fasted alone in a house that didn't understand Islam… He saw you.

When you sat in sajdah and cried without words… He was close.

Always.

"And He is with you wherever you are." (Qur'an 57:4)

What Comes Next?

More growth.

More tests.

More du'as you don't yet know you'll make.

More moments where you feel so close to Allah you can almost hear your heartbeat say *alhamdulillah*.

And yes — more setbacks.

More missed prayers.

More tears.

More questions.

More "I thought I was past this" moments.

But here's the gift:

You've already learned how to return.

You've learned how to breathe through the guilt.

You've learned how to reach for Allah in the quiet.

You've learned how to forgive yourself.

You've learned how to whisper, *"Guide me..."* and trust that He will.

You're not starting from scratch anymore.

You're building something sacred — slowly, patiently, day by day.

The Seasons Will Change

There will be seasons where your iman feels high — where salah is sweet and the Qur'an speaks to you with every page.

There will be seasons where it's harder to feel anything — where you recite with a dry tongue and distracted thoughts.

Both are normal.

Both are part of the path.

Faith is like the moon.

Sometimes full.

Sometimes hidden.

But always present — always circling back to light.

And Allah is never distant.

Even when you feel far from Him — He is close.

Even when you feel numb — He is still listening.

Even when you're not sure how to return — He is still holding the door open.

"Indeed, My mercy encompasses all things." (Qur'an 7:156)

Even you. Even now. Even always.

You Are Part of Something Bigger

As a revert, it can sometimes feel like you're on the outside of a faith that was never meant to be yours. But here's the truth:

This ummah needs you.

It needs your perspective.

It needs your resilience.

It needs your compassion.

It needs your reminders that Allah guides whom He wills — and that guidance is a gift, not a right.

You are proof of His mercy.

You are living da'wah.

You are loved — by your Lord and by countless others who are walking this road with you, even if you haven't met them yet.

Never forget that.

A Final Du'a to Carry in Your Heart

"Ya Allah, thank You for bringing me to Islam. Thank you for walking beside me every step of the way. When I doubted, You steadied me. When I cried, You held me. When I fell, You waited for me to rise again. Keep me close. Keep me sincere. Keep me Yours — always."

Ameen.

As you close the final page of this book, I want you to take a deep breath.

You've walked through your first prayers, your first tests, your first joys, and your first doubts. You've sat with your heart, reflected on your journey, and whispered du'as that only Allah knows. And through it all, you've been growing — quietly, beautifully — in ways that aren't always visible to the eye but are deeply known to the One who sees your soul.

This isn't the end. This is a pause — a still moment before your next steps.

May Allah continue to anchor you in peace, surround you with sincere support, and open doors of healing, love, and understanding. And may you always remember even when the world feels noisy and uncertain, the stillness after shahada is where you can always return. *Ameen.*

A Gentle Whisper Forward

~~~

To the one holding this book in your hands, thank you for walking through these pages with your heart open.

You may have come to Islam with trembling hands or with quiet certainty. You may have stumbled or soared. But through it all, you chose Allah. Again and again. That is beautiful. That is brave.

Stillness After Shahada was written for the moments in between—the ones no one sees but Allah. The tears on your prayer mat. The silence after doubt. The longing for belonging. The tiny victories that felt enormous in your soul. All of it matters.

Let this book be a soft companion, not a finish line. Your journey doesn't end here. It begins anew, every day, with each intention, each act of worship, each whispered du'a. Allah is with you—in your struggles, in your growth, in your return to Him.

And whenever you forget, come back. Come back to the stillness. Come back to the remembrance. Come back to your heart.

From one revert soul to another, with all my love and du'a,

Joyful Hijabi

Printed in Dunstable, United Kingdom